WAKE UP & BE AWESOME

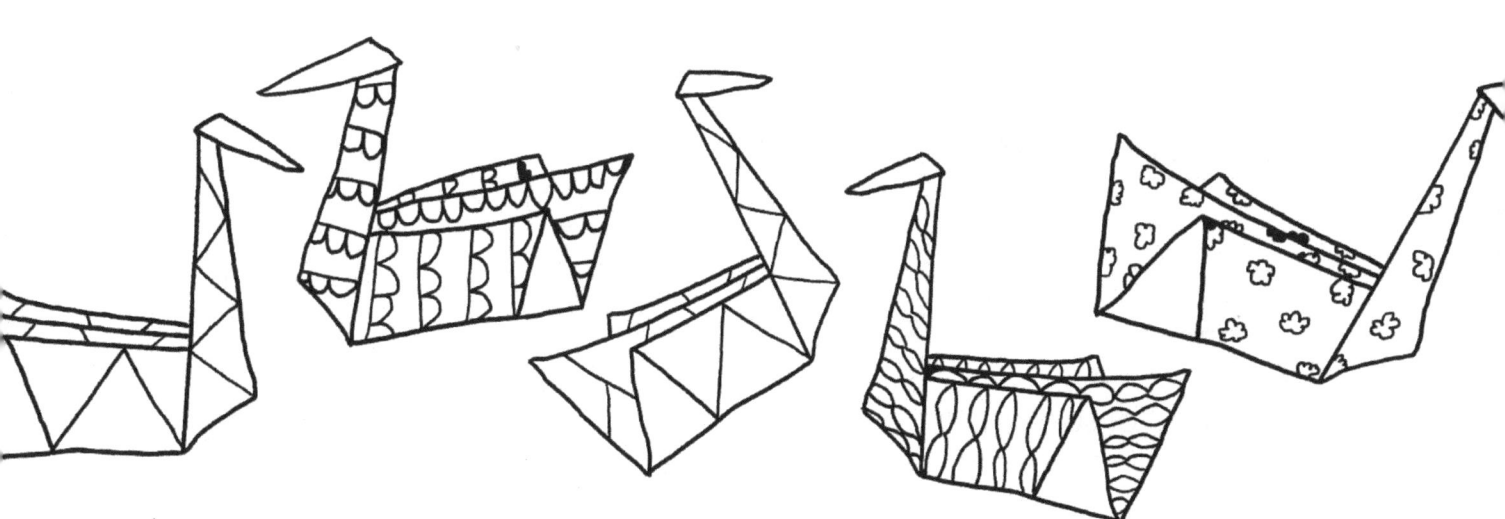

OH, SUSANNAH®

Published in 2016 by
Oh, Susannah®
Greensboro, NC
email: info@ohsusannah.com
www.ohsusannah.com

All rights reserved. No part of this publication may be reproduced or transmitted in any form or by any means, electronic or mechanical, including photocopy, recording, or any information storage and retreieval system, without permission in writing from the publisher.

ISBN: 978-0692809488

WAKE UP & BE AWESOME

A MOTIVATIONAL COLORING BOOK

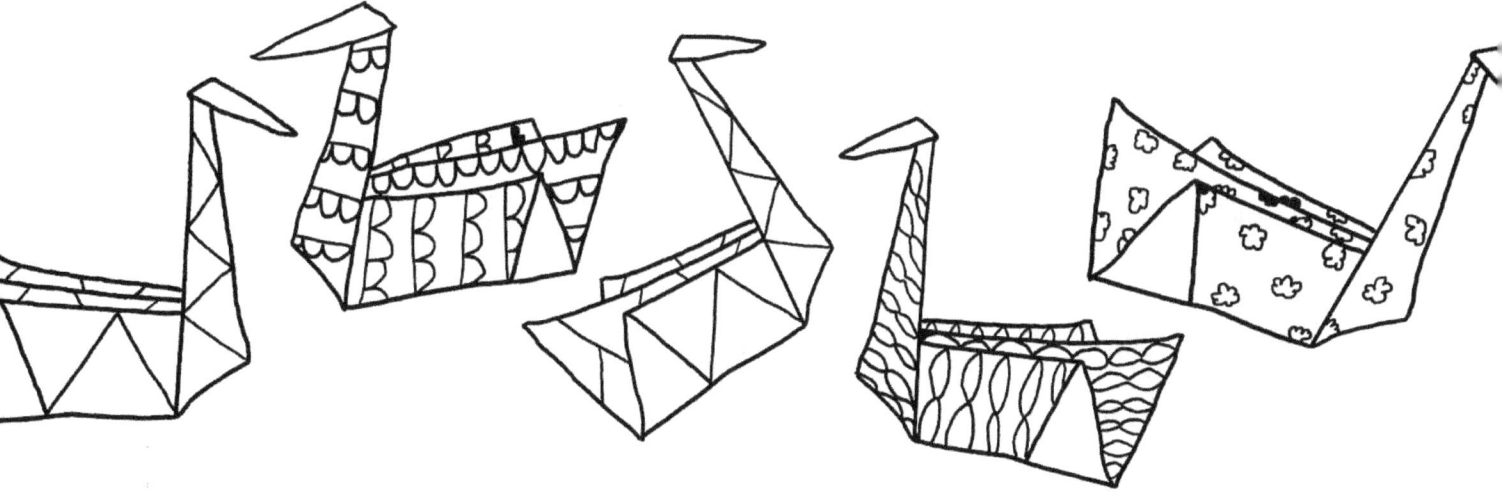

BY
Susannah O'Brien

ILLUSTRATED BY
Betsy Petersen

bonjour!

Trailing „What's your favorite color?" in popularity for top questions to kids is, „What do you want to be when you grow up?" As an adult my answer would be, „Who says I want to grow up?" but as a child, my answer was that I wanted to be an author and illustrate my own books. I was inspired by one of my earliest teachers, Mr. O'Keefe, who recognized the importance of imagination in education. He set aside time every day for creative writng, helped us bind our own novelas with patterned papaer, and then gathered us around to hear each other's stories. He was wonderful. It only took me 20 years to publish a book, and Mr. O'Keefe may be disappointed to discover I developed no artistic talent in all these years. Instead I have asked my incredibly talented siser-in-law, Betsy Petersen, to illustrate my ideas. Together, we are so excited to present this book to you!

This book was inspired by my son. I'd only known very friendly, outgoing children before he was born, so it came as a shock to have a child who prefers to be left alone, likes familiar places, and demands order and control. He has a very systematic mind and follows his own set of rules that govern his behavior. It has been hard for me to watch him struggle socially around other kids, adults, and even family members, but I've come to accept that he'll never be the sort of kid to come home from school, and into my arms with a big hug and kiss, and gush about his day. Though his ambivalence towards life makes me sad sometimes, ultimately we're like every other parent/ child duo: I just want him to be happy.

It is my sincere belief that art is an underrated therapeutic tool we can use to engage with children. It is while absentmindedly coloring that my son begins to open up to me and I see the potential of his imagination. He is suddenly silly, whimsical, and full of life. This book takes the act of drawing one step further with inspirational content. Pages featuring sentiments like "Never Grow Up," "Wake Up And Be Awesome," and "Go Get 'Em, Tiger" are not only fun to color, but also encourage children to go beyond their comfort zones and stay positive. Other pages are designed with fun images like donuts, pizza, and paper airplanes to help kids recognize and appreciate the simple joys in life. You'll also find entrancing patterns throughout the book, meant to ease the busy mind of anxious children and help anyone relax. Opposite the coloring pages are motivatonal thoughts you can read and consider with your child as they draw. This combination can help them think more deeply about the messages our coloring pages send.

Not only are these beautiful images you can have fun coloring togehter, but they are specially formatted as 8" x 10" pages that you can tear out, frame, and dislay around the house. As with every other lesson we parents teach, repetition is key. A message like "Wake Up And Be Awesome" will mean something to a child while it's being colored, more if a parent discusses the message, and still more if they see their artwork on a regular basis.

Many of the images and quotes found in this book were inspired by the designs on our original product: pillow cases. Our initial goal was to provide a way for kids to feel happy as they went to sleep and inspired as they awoke, and I'm thriled that we can now encouarge children throughout the day. For more information on inspiring home products visit our website, found in the back of the book.

I hope your family loves this book as much as we do!

-Susannah

Chocolate frosted, jelly filled, glazed...
Just like people, donuts come in lots of wonderful shapes and sizes.
You'll never know which you like the best unless you
try them all!

Do you ever feel like your brain is buzzing? It's not bees in there, it's all of your thoughts, feelings, and questions.
Sometimes you need to give your beautiful brain a break!
Focus on these magic lines and let your mind relax as your daily thinks melt away...

Sieze the day! What can you do to make today a great day?

A hero isn't just someone who fights crime, a hero is anyone who tries to make the world a better place. If you play with someone who is lonely or help someone in need you are a hero, too!

Don't be afraid to color outside of the lines!
Let your mind wander and your hand do what comes
naturally. There's no right or wrong way
to color!

Eventually you'll get older, but that doesn't mean you'll have to give up the things you love now. Even adults still dance, sing, laugh, and color!

Have you ever made a paper airplane?
Try folding any piece of paper unti it flies,
then see how far you can make it go!
Old school papers, the grocery list, or junk mail
all have some magic left in them.

Which things bring you the most joy?
What does your happy place look like?

Bonjour! Hola! Hallo! Ciao! Hello!
Whether it's in French, Spanish, Dutch, Italian, English,
or any other language, it only takes one word
to make a new friend!

bonjour

bonjour

bonjour

bonjour

What is your favorite animal?
Would you like to live with one?
What would you do together?

You can.

YES!
YES! YES!
YES! YES!
YES! YES!
YES! YES!
YES!

Pandas inspire tranquility, strength, and determination.
What wonderful qualities!

The only thing you can control is your attitude.
Will you decide to be happy, or
choose to be unhappy?
(Being happy is so much more fun.)

Origami cranes are a symbol of happiness and peace. You can be a peacemaker by forgiving someone who hurt you, or apologizing if you hurt someone else.

One person may see hills and valleys,
another a sunrise or waves.
We're all a little different, and that's what
makes everyone special.
You have to figure out what it means to you!

If you choose to see the good in all things,
even the weather becomes beautiful and fun.
Snow is a clean, fresh blanket, flashes
of lightening start dancing across the sky,
wind invisibly whispers through the trees, and
even rain becomes a giant sprinkler.

It's one of those things you can only do for yourself.
So if you don't, who will?

It's ok if you suddenly like brocolli or if orange becomes your new favorite color. Even the moon changes every day.

There are too many stars in the sky to count.
Together, they form the bigger picture.
Isn't it wonderful that something
so small can be part of something so grand?

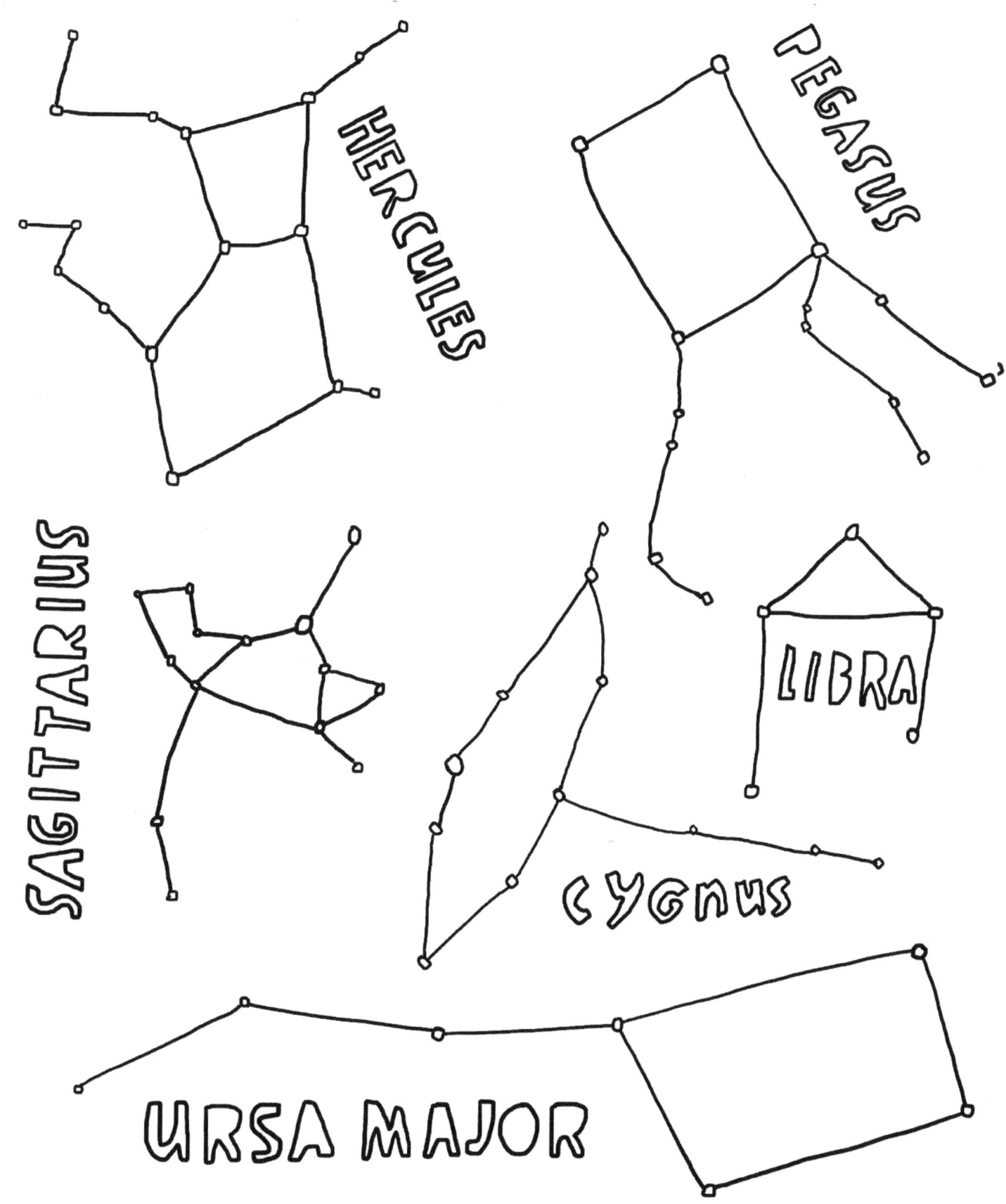

DRAW WHAT MAKES YOU HAPPY HERE...

DRAW WHAT MAKES YOU HAPPY HERE...

DRAW WHAT MAKES YOU HAPPY HERE...

DRAW WHAT MAKES YOU HAPPY HERE...

betsypetersen.com

OH, SUSANNAH®

I like you & naps.

you're, like, really pretty.

bonjour

DREAM big

LA VIE -C'EST- BON

just one more chapter...

WAKE UP AND BE AWESOME

Head to www.ohsusannah.com for more inspirational home products and free coloring pages!

www.ingramcontent.com/pod-product-compliance
Lightning Source LLC
Chambersburg PA
CBHW080943040426
42444CB00015B/3424